The Art of Delegation: Maximize Your Time, Leverage Others, and Instantly Increase Profits

Disclaimer and Terms of Use: Effort has been made to ensure that the information in this book is accurate and complete, however, the author and the publisher do not warrant the accuracy of the information, text and graphics contained within the book due to the rapidly changing nature of science, research, known and unknown facts and internet. The Author and the publisher do not hold any responsibility for errors, omissions or contrary interpretation of the subject matter herein. This book is presented solely for motivational and informational purposes only.

Table of Contents

Introduction
Empowerment

Empowering & Delegating

Delegating to workplace subordinates involves granting authority down the ranks and giving those being commissioned the tools, skills and knowledge to be effective and successful. For proper delegating to occur, those two steps are inseparable. If you delegate without empowering, i.e. give someone a task without also giving them the knowledge and means to accomplish it successfully, you would be merely adding to their stress and misery. Part of delegating therefore includes coaching and mentoring, but also the boosting of the empowered person's self-confidence, courage and sharing in the significance of the task being handed down.

Subordinate employees can thus come out feeling liberated, able to make their own choices and in charge of their self-image since they have been made responsible for something meaningful that others will partake in.

As long as such co-workers perceive that doing their job satisfies important needs of in-house colleagues or external customers, they'll have a positive perception of the meaningfulness of their work. Employees must thus feel like they are able to influence people and events in important ways in order to feel empowered.

Empowerment goes much farther than that though, in or outside of the workplace. Inspired people who empower others routinely and without a fuss are viewed as belonging to the "good people" who have great inner fortitude and awareness. They are kind, their empathy boundless, and they invariably become influential mentors.

Empowerment can take the shape of praise, or a nod or smile that confirms appreciation or even simple acknowledgment. It is necessary when delegating down as we've described, but you don't need to delegate in order to empower.

The biggest event in a homeless person's day could easily be, as an example, if a seemingly successful person extends his or her arm for a hand shake, or if they're merely asked how their day is going, or given a greeting with a smile.

As you grow, you enlarge your circle of family, friends and acquaintances. You get involved in hundreds –thousands throughout a life cycle- of rapport building and new relationships. With that groundswell of connections, the influence you wield increases, and your choice becomes a simple one: how will you choose to exercise that influence?

Many people choose to be generous towards others and empower them as opportunities arise. That becomes a mantra for them, a way of life, a philosophy and a doctrine, a life companion and a collection of self-regulating instincts that become etched on their subconscious mind. If you've recently come across someone like that –perhaps a teacher- you will appreciate that you are truly free when you hug this mantra, when the difference between right and wrong may be in everyone else's mind –hardly ever in yours.

You will notice that we are also describing empathy, again. The dictionary defines empathy as "the capacity to recognize emotions that are being experienced by another being." Empathy is the precursor of love and compassion. It is the bedrock foundation that sets the tone for empowerment.

When you empower someone you don't criticize them, and you don't judge them. You restrain your natural egotistical tendencies as well as any vestiges of cynicism that you may have. You put on your genuinely kindest robes and you find something nice to say to the other person. You let the other person soak in the best traits that you have garnered, and you do all that without a fuss.

At the end of the day, your words may be forgotten, and your actions too, but those with whom you had such encounters will never forget you.

Empowerment is not to be confused with delegating, although some of the guiding principles are similar for both. You can empower a branch manager and set them free to do your bidding, only using their own methods. You don't have to transfer actual tasks to them as you would if you were delegating precise assignments. In our fast-paced workplace these days, there may not be sufficient time for a truly busy manager to sit and bolster someone's mindset before giving them a chore. The busy manager may also not be too familiar with the art of empowerment. The delegating may thus come without empowerment, unless of course the empowerment preceded the delegating. For example, the manager holds a team meeting in which his goal is entirely about empowerment and morale boosting. At the end of the meeting, the manager may sit with one person and briefly delegate a task.

This delegating process has become more than just an art these days, and we will be examining what it entails in detail in subsequent parts of this book.

Finally, having an empowered group of employees reporting to you is every leader's dream. It means they don't have to be nudged every time there are important assignments to be undertaken, and you can expect them to take initiatives and perform in manners consistent with your –or your company's- values and policies.

When you have not sufficiently empowered such employees, you risk ending up spending an unwarranted amount of time micro-managing all the little steps they need to take. The most enlightened managers create within their team an environment of empowerment with individual team members taking ownership of their work and holding themselves accountable.

~   ~   ~

Chapter One
Self-Confidence

In order to delegate effectively, our premise in this chapter is that you need to continually take stock of your managerial methods and possess an abundant hoard of self-confidence and courage.

Upward Self-Revisions

A recent study out of Ohio State University sheds light on the critical role that self-confidence plays in propelling you on a stellar career path. Not only is your success in the workplace predicated upon possessing a healthy dose of self-confidence, but you also need to have that confidence validated every now and then by your peers in general and your co-workers and bosses in particular.

The study sets forth the notion that if you can visualize yourself in a future setting as the successful business person that you want to be, that such future visions tend to make your goals more attainable. This is called "upward self-revision", an exercise in periodically reassessing yourself on an upward career trajectory, and it is based on your innermost ambitions. And although such revisions are naturally kept in check by your sense of practical realities, they nevertheless play a role in at least keeping you from falling behind in your quest for valuable self-confidence. For those who have great talent but lack self-confidence in pursuit of a dream, upward self-revisions can yield useful rewards.

In exploring some personal development traits that affect your ability to delegate effectively, high among those is the self-confidence that is necessary to look beyond yourself and to see the many benefits of delegating.

Self-confidence is like a drip-drip infusion of adrenalin. It makes you believe in yourself and opens up wonderful capacities for rapport and relationship building, perception, creative functioning, calibrated venturing, love, vitality, awareness and more. And the beauty of self-confidence is that it is not something you are born with, but something, that you can develop and nurture (more on that in subsequent sections).

Although self-confidence is different from self-esteem, the two diverge only fractionally. For example, celebrities can be thoroughly confident when in the limelight but have low self-esteem when by themselves. A football player can be in the top echelon of stars in his position and yet go home after the game and feel unworthy. It is also possible –though unlikely- to think highly of yourself (self-esteem) and yet not have the confidence to experiment and be creative at the office.

The distinctions between self-confidence and self-esteem are small enough for us to keep for another day. Instead, we can concentrate on self-confidence as embodying one of the essential prerequisites for effective delegating.

Self-Confidence

Self-confidence is the common yardstick by which you evaluate yourself, the essential ingredient in that evaluation consisting of a feeling of being competent to deal with whatever comes up.

The incubators for that feeling are your particular skills and your "fluid" intelligence, i.e. your ability –your alacrity- at interacting well with your environment, including that environment's endless amalgam of complex circumstances, people, unforeseen events and self-inflicted setbacks.

Self-confidence also has a tinge of "worthiness", which is more subjective and therefore more challenging. For example, what are you meant to be worthy of? Are you meant to be worthy of society's acceptance, happiness, having the best family, doing great professionally, a leadership role in your community, material wellbeing?

Thus self-confidence entails the marks that you give yourself in terms of your general capabilities as well as society's validation of such marks. If you want your self-confidence to remain primed and expedient, you need to receive society's pat on the back every now and again. It is a validation of your smarts and clever adeptness that you may have a great deal of attachment to.

But you can tell that it's not as simple as that, for both those elements –self-confidence and validation- are impacted considerably by your culture, faith, society's fads and factors like stereo-typing, stigmas, guilt, upbringing, environmental and behavioral issues, and more.

For example, your self-confidence is developed within a certain geography and environment, where your familiarity with your surroundings plays an important role. You feel you can cope with whatever comes at you more effectively within the confines of your everyday setting. Thus if you were to move from the US to India, for example, much of the nurturing of your abilities and the validations you receive from your American society may not be of help in India.

Does that mean that your self-confidence depends on where you find yourself at any given time? Does the same logic apply when you move from one trade or employer to another? One group of friends to a new one, younger/older, more/less sophisticated?

Your environment has a lot to say with regard to how you feel about yourself, and your environment is not always predictable. It behooves you therefore to work at boosting your self-confidence (next section), so that you can wage your battles from a position of strength.

Self-confidence is a delicate –frequently tantalizing- measure of how you are doing. Too much of it conjures up self-aggrandizement and arrogance, while too little of it beckons all kinds of problems, including fear, self-recrimination and different degrees of paralysis.

It is self-confidence which is considered the overarching driver of success in Western cultures. The reasoning has it that you must absolutely have a high assessment of yourself in order to get anywhere in a career. For example, can a sales person with poor self-confidence make cold calls? Can they be effective at closing on deals? Can a department head with low self-confidence wield the necessary degree of influence on people in other departments over whom he or she has no formal authority? Can someone with questionable self-confidence go up on a stage and make a presentation in front of 500 people?

From another perspective, no matter how brilliant you are, there are always people who are more brilliant, and no matter how hard you try, there are always people who seem to attain the same results with less effort. There is always someone better looking, taller, richer, more eloquent and a higher-echelon leader. In fact, when the mood is such that you turn hard on yourself, it is easy for you to perceive that there is always someone doing better than you and who makes you feel like a failure, and failure is forbidden when you're coasting on self-confidence. Failure, even temporary setbacks, risks to bring down the house of cards.

Besides, when you attain self-confidence, you have to maintain it, which can be a struggle at the best of times. As such, you must keep stroking your ego and feeling that you are totally amazing, and then you must maintain that high mental image of yourself, for fear that any misstep could set you back.

Self-compassion, i.e. self-acceptance or self-love, is a great addendum to self-confidence. Self-compassion is malleable, easier on the soul, more amenable to a prompt rebound after a setback and an all-in-all better key to unlocking your potential. It embodies a fundamental willingness to treat yourself kindly when in doubt, or having made mistakes. It then prompts you to slowly work yourself out of the hole –compassionately. In study after study, research has shown that self-compassion is a great conduit to a personal sense of wellbeing and happiness.

"Well," you might say to yourself, "I can't make cold calls. I never have." But the idea is that you accept that of yourself –compassionately- and determine to practice making cold calls until you improve at it –if, that is, it's meant for you to make cold calls. Your self-compassion played a critical role there in motivating you to do what you had to do, and in further boosting your confidence factor.

In this line of thinking, self-compassion, as an add-on to self-confidence, goes beyond achievement and the workplace, to a whole new realm of goodness and happiness. Self-compassion thus becomes the anchor for the balance you strive to attain in your life. Since you accept yourself compassionately, it probably follows that you accept others as well in the same manner, and that you are an optimist with an outgoing personality, all necessary ingredients for a well equilibrated approach to life.

In the same tests that researchers conducted, the people with self-compassion viewed their weaknesses as areas that they were going to work on with the view to creating improvements.

There was neither acceptance of their weaknesses nor of their poor output but, instead, there was resolve, with compassion, to improve. This determination would lead to greater work quality, rather than to a deterioration of self-confidence.

10 Ways to Boost your Self-Confidence

1. **Bring changes to your thought patterns**: The starting point is to shed any negative self-images and persistent thoughts you may have accumulated, irrespective of their origin. With total resolve, you have to view this ridding yourself of all negativity as a foundational base from which self-confidence can rise. If you are to believe that you are not worthy, not intelligent enough, and that you can never amount to much, then that will naturally become a self-prophecy.

2. **Bring changes to your daily habits**: every negative facet that you encounter about yourself has to be dealt with. For example, if you are tentative and hesitant when you speak, isolate that weakness, examine it, compare it to your observations of how other people speak, and

deal with it by resolving to make a conscious effort to improve. Similarly, other characteristics of your feelings, personality, skills, performance at work and interaction with people have to be examined and worked at.

3. **Adopt "fitness for life":** with exercise and fitness, you (and particularly your skin) will acquire a new glow that points at good health and athleticism, highly regarded traits and magnets for your friends and co-workers. Another immediate benefit from making those lifestyle adaptations is that you acquire an athletic posture, a great part of how you want to be perceived. Learn to always walk without a slouch and with your head held high. Learn to move about naturally like that, so that your personal gait will come effortlessly to you when in company.

4. **Work on your overall appearance:** we often reflect on how a 20-minute run can improve how you feel about yourself, but so can good grooming and looking after your appearance

generally, particularly in the choice of clothes that you wear. If you're not much good as a style consultant, seek a relative or friend whose taste you always liked and ask them simply to help you work on your selection of clothes. Soon you will start looking at yourself in the mirror and liking what you see, which helps boost your self-confidence.

5. **Self-confidence stems from self-love:** teach yourself to stand tall inside your mind, and let that superior love fill you up with a positive outlook. Think of yourself as coming from the same source as all the people for whom you have high regard. Life shaped you a little differently up to this point in time, and you can shape yourself any way you want from this point on –as long as you embrace your self-compassion and keep your focus on the positive.

Your past does not determine your future, and your future starts right now. In addition, your newly found self-confidence will be acknowledged by those around you, and they will

start treating you with more admiration. You will
have embarked on a journey that will take you
all the way to wherever you aspire to go.

6. **Externalize and offer your services:** we get
too cooped up in our little world, preoccupied
with the zillion thought patterns that cross our
minds continually, usually just gibberish that we
somehow get entangled with. So break that
pattern and bust out to see "what else there is"
out there. One of the good ways to keep the
mind fresh is to step outside of your comfort
zone and go find out if there is anyone that you
could help today. In the workplace, there are
endless ways you could be of help to someone,
and your reward will always be unquestionably
fulfilling.

7. **Be mindful of how you communicate**: try to
listen intently to one or two inspirational
speakers (their videos are easily accessible). Also
try to view and listen to a TED-speaker (there
are nearly 2000 TED-speakers on many diverse
subjects, the common denominator between

them being the excellence of the speakers). "TED-talks" (they can be googled like that) are remarkably smart, incisive, and the presentation is usually amazing. The point is that you would benefit from concentrating on your listening habits and how you speak, i.e. your voice, the clarity of your thoughts, and the endless mannerisms that your body language projects when you're in conversation. In each case, think of someone you admire, and try to examine why they do something or other better than you.

8. **Acknowledge and compliment others:** we discussed the validation needed from others in order to reinforce one's self-confidence, but bestowing someone else with a compliment, or even simply acknowledging them with eye contact and a smile, is itself rewarding. To be self-confident, yet humble and generous at heart, is a worthy goal.

9. **Work at being the best in your field:** you may not be 6'4" or have a powerhouse head of hair, but you certainly can get known to be good

–an authority– in what you do. Your expertise, together with your other faculties, will again act as a magnate both in the office as well as more generally in life. And you will also be inclined to tutor and mentor others which is helpful as well.

10. **Keep your stress under control:** stress is a malignant force that can cause significant damage to your mental and physical wellbeing. Fight it with the healthy lifestyle that was above described, but also fight it by being outgoing, networking with new people, socializing with friends whenever you can and taking up a stress-relief modality such as visualization, yoga, meditation, breathing and other.

~   ~   ~

Chapter two
Why you should Delegate

Why delegate?

Many startup entrepreneurs embark on their ventures by personally taking on the hundreds of tasks that come up around the office on a daily basis. They cannot afford to do it any other way, for they simply don't have the staff, and they can achieve Herculean miracles in this manner –as long as the volume of business remains relatively small.

It's a different story however when their business starts growing, and when they can afford to start adding staff. If they continue with their habit of doing everything themselves, they will sooner or later hit a wall of frustration and helplessness. The smarter entrepreneurs will not waste time before they start building one or more teams comprising team members who can be taught to undertake a whole slew of functions. Many tasks and business management responsibilities can thus be delegated, enabling the boss to pursue the business's higher objectives.

Naturally, smart executives can manifest their savvy in many ways, although one of those critical methods is to learn and practice effective delegating. As a manager, the function of delegating itself is complex and demanding of your best effort. You might easily experience that despite delegating a task as best as you know how, you still face frustrations. Either the task ends up not being done completely or on time, or the staff members you delegated to keep coming back with a string of questions and displaying confusion. When that happens, you may wish that you'd done the task yourself and have been spared the aggravations.

As successful startup entrepreneurs grow, they quickly learn to let go of a plurality of their tasks. They learn that they can only rise up by delegating down. And when they communicate to their subordinates that the destiny of the organization is in their hands, they are able to build motivated teams to take on responsibilities in an accountable environment.

Managers, more so than the higher up executives, frequently feel loath to hand over important tasks to team members. They commonly embrace the illusion of believing that they –and only they- can accomplish something in the way that it should be done. To corroborate their case, they turn perfectionist, and when that happens it's easy enough to find fault with whatever someone else does. They point at tiny details that were imperceptibly "sub-standard", and from that they make the case that the entire chore that was delegated was a failure –and not to be repeated.

Such managers may simply not know how to delegate effectively. They never bothered to teach themselves, and no one ever taught or mentored them, on the art of delegating. They harbor old fashioned notions that become significant impediments to successful management. Here are a few examples of their mindset:

- It's a lot less complicated and faster to just go ahead and do the chores myself
- I am convinced that my bosses want me to do things myself

- I don't mind doing things myself; in fact it keeps me busy, and I enjoy it
- I don't have the time to teach someone in one sitting everything I learned over years about a particular task
- What are the merits of handing over a task to someone else if I then have to sit and correct what they've done over and over again?
- So what if I have to work long hours and weekends to stay on top of everything? I am prepared to do that, and my bosses like that in me
- It would seem like I would be asking for help, and that's not like me –I prefer to rely on myself rather than put my fate in the hands of others
- And the ultimate reason is the fear that those to whom I delegate would become equally proficient as me and eventually take my job

For a start, it's easy to recognize that one person –any person- can quickly become a bottleneck and major drain on the organization if they embrace a mindset like that. Simply put, you would be standing in the way of progress if you choose to burn yourself out by sinking into a sea of chores and details. Leaders lead, and managers manage, so learn to assume your position as leader of an effective team, and share the workload.

~   ~   ~

Chapter Three
Benefits of Delegating

Essential Tasks of Team Leaders

One of the essential tasks of team leaders is to obtain results from their team members. If they don't, they might as well be playing tennis with one hand tied behind their back.

And yet many managers struggle with the idea of delegation, or they may have gotten into their positions of leadership without any background in delegating. For example, a great sales person is catapulted into the position of sales manager, the assumption being that if he excelled at sales, he would do equally well as a team leader –a proposition that is highly suspect. He might have the right work ethic and be otherwise well qualified, but in sales he would have spent his entire career fending for himself, with no team members to look after. If one is to succeed as a team leader and produce results, getting an education in the art of delegation is an absolute must.

Here is why:

10 Benefits that Result from Delegating

1. **Your time:** delegating tasks is liberating in its nature. As you cross off chores from your "to do" list, you end up with increased opportunities to pursue the strategic thinking that you never had the time for before. This would include such essential functions as planning, organizing and providing additional team support to your bosses. Imagine how much more you could achieve if you could lighten up your workload, and imagine the added benefits you could bring to your team and your organization if you weren't tied up every day in tasks that could be accomplished by others.

2. **Your crew:** when you empower one or more of your team members, you unlock their pent up

abilities and hidden talents. In delegating, you are in essence assigning to them tasks and goals that up to then had been beyond their job description. You would be asking them to extend themselves and give you efforts that had not been a part of their routine duties. You would share in your own learning and experience, thus enhancing their skillsets, and you would make them accountable, thus elevating their self-esteem.

3. **Empowerment:** nothing like empowerment to see a favorable transformation among team members. The act of delegation entails indirectly telling a subordinate employee that you respect their ability to learn and perform satisfactorily, and that you trust them to act judiciously and in the best interest of the company. Enabled like that, you get from them a greater level of commitment to the task on hand, to the company, and to their team leader. Add to that the fact that teaching subordinates more about the company and its products puts subordinates ever closer to having direct contact with higher-

ups in the company as well as outside customers. This inevitably results in team members taking ownership of what they've been asked to do, when nothing works better than team members striving to improve customer satisfaction.

4. **Your leadership:** for team members to have utmost respect for you, you would need to sharpen such traits as integrity, clarity of thought and voice, and a sense of fair play and empathy for your co-workers –all pillars of leadership. This will set you on your path to wielding influence beyond the workplace. Whether you're proficient at it or not, delegation at the onset reinforces in you how to develop and manage your team more efficiently. This learning is a core byproduct of managing delegation artfully, and the rewards that ensue become incentives that propel you towards more refinement in delegation. A good example is the surprise that you will promptly experience at the speed with which your team rises to the

occasion, and team productivity shoots up.

5. **New ways of doing things:** When you assign a task to someone else and make sure that they are equipped to successfully achieving it, it invariably brings to light new ways of doing it, ways that you'd been following for several years. Delegation thus gets you outside of your habitual methods when your team member gets a shot at discovering an innovation, new twist or shortcut to your old process.

6. **Delegation benefits your organization:** when the environment at work is one of trust, and employee morale is high, and when everyone is aware of the productivity factor and working towards greater efficiencies, the organization is the ultimate benefactor. A culture of creativity and enthusiasm fosters team cohesion, teamwork and ingenuity. Employees are less likely to leave the organization, and the organization ends up with better trained employees and better honed

skills.

7. **Your chance to focus:** chances are you've never put yourself through the test –until you've started to delegate. Your own pent up abilities finally get a chance to flourish when, that is, you get a break from being swamped with work, and you can "smell the roses". You can finally concentrate on what you're really good at, particularly on being a great team leader. Your team can now be a lot more productive, but your own contribution may also reach heights that may be unexpected. Given the opportunity to focus and carry the good thoughts forward in newly liberated strategic thinking, you may even begin to discover what you are capable of.

8. **Your skills:** delegation is a process that involves taking several steps with your selected team members. Because you don't want to lose their time or yours, you need to do extensive planning. You need to first know precisely who among your team members you want to assign a task or project to. In view of some employees'

skillsets, this might be an easy task, but if, on the other hand, you have never been practiced at meaningful delegating in the past, then it's time to assess and be selective. You have to explain with clarity what the task involves, how it has been done in the past, and whatever possible obstacles might be encountered. You have to ensure that your team member is assimilating all that you are saying, and that they comprehend the review points you have designed. In this process, you have sharpened your communication skills, planning, and employee assessment faculty.

9. **New horizons for the team:** the team eventually begins to function solidly as one entity while at the same time offering you a variety of newly developed skills. The talent pool has undergone significant expansion, including specializations that did not previously exist. These might be in software, copywriting, marketing, accounting, project management, supply chains, and many other fields. You therefore now have the potential of undertaking

new activities that were previously out of reach, with a newly acquired competitive edge.

10. Your future is promising: if you've managed to transform your unit into a successful machine, you're probably also capable of doing the same at the level of a larger unit, or of the company itself, and astute delegating was at the heart of your accomplishments. You now have leverage in any direction, even pathways that had previously been out of question for your team. What you did, perhaps on a small scale within your team, is the same as you might be asked to do in a more senior position in your company.

~   ~   ~

Chapter Four
The Process of Delegation

Prepare to Delegate

If you're suddenly embarking on delegation, it's usually because you and your team have been in a rut, your performance dull and unproductive. You blame yourself or, worse, your supervisors are showing signs of frustration, and action is clearly warranted.

But it's not easy, and the barriers to effective delegation are numerous. For starters, you have to slow your operation down sufficiently to give you time to think strategically and to create a master plan. Your plan would set objectives and standards and would call for assessing the specific capabilities of your employees and developing interim review points and achievement metrics that your team members can understand. A comprehensive plan would also have you involving your team members in the delegation process and informing other team members when you start delegating to one or two employees.

Above all, you have to decide on what you want to delegate, and it is recommended in that context that you take baby steps, assigning the easier tasks first. Don't forget, together with your subordinates, you will be on a learning curve, so you want to take steps that don't bring the roof down if people –including you- make mistakes.

From the beginning though, delegate those recurring activities that will be part of your subordinate's future responsibility. Thus in essence you are beginning to match individual talent with long term activities. In this respect, your own activities might be kept for functions like reviews, coaching, mentoring and helping out with the more complex or sensitive issues, such as people's wages and interactions with the higher-ups.

Here are more details about the delegation process:

10 Guidelines for Successful Delegation

1. **The right frame of mind**: you've selected a few easy chores of the repetitive kind, and you have established in your mind who you want to delegate them to. It's time now to shed the thinking that only you can get something done correctly. On the contrary, think that someone else might do an even better job on a specific task. In fact, in your new frame of mind you are going to do everything within your power to get each subordinate perform at your level or better. Just enjoy your newly found freedom from all those boring tasks that you'll now unload.

2. **Be decisive and firm**: in the past, when team members came to you offering their help, you turned them down. It's time now that you wield your influence and take control, mostly by being firm, but also by being adequately prepared. You can't dump something that is ill conceived on a subordinate and hope that they'll put their

heart to it and produce worthy results. Having made plans that involve specific subordinates, go and get them, one by one, without giving them too much of an option. Delegating requires the team's collaboration, so be the leader that can get that going without too much trouble. If you're uncomfortable asking for someone's cooperation and help, then you have to get over it. Without asking you won't get, and you would remain mired with a debilitating workload.

3. **Build a culture of trust**: Some managers feel that they can be kinder with their employees – give them less work. In fact, by delegating, you are teaching tasks that you've been doing for a long time, and you're mentoring your subordinates and showing them all the intricate ways that you developed for doing something or other in a more efficient way. You are thus giving them new skills, so why would you feel inadequate at loading them with all the chores that you think they can accomplish with good results. The issue of trust has to be the cornerstone of your handling of the delegation

process. You have to trust –and verify- that they give you their best effort, and they have to trust that you are not just delegating without senselessly.

4. **Be clear when delegating**: explain, in as clear a manner as you can, exactly what you want your subordinates to do, and especially the responsibilities that you are empowering them with. Don't give up on this critical step until you are certain that you've been understood, and that they've accepted your terms. Try to strike the perfect balance between giving so much detail that your helper feels insulted and not giving enough for your helper to get a good grasp of your assignment.

5. **Delegate the task, not your mindset**: keep your motives and philosophy to yourself early in the delegating process, and when passing on a task, set the performance standards for it, i.e. your expectations in terms of the level of excellence that your subordinate should deliver. Explain your objectives behind the chore,

ensuring that they are attainable, and that your employee understands how you will be evaluating results. In addition, be sure to transfer to your employee all the authority and tools that they will need in their new responsibilities. At times this authority might entail paying out of company funds, consulting with others within or outside of the team, and speaking for or negotiating on behalf of the team or the company.

6. **Fight the temptation to micro-manage**: You would need to show your subordinate how to do the task, though you would want to stay clear of being a "control-freak". Leave the employee some room for discovery, telling them they can do it in their own way if they prefer, as long that the task is done on time and up to set standards. If that doesn't go well for you, or if the employee gets stuck, keep in mind that you will have occasion to check on progress at key intervals. Instead of stifling their effort with frustrating play-by-play descriptions, give your subordinates the latitude to be creative and

experiment, and enjoy your own fewer "to do" chores and more free time.

7. **Train, mentor and coach**: a team member may take some time and effort to train, but remember, this is a long term investment for you and your company. You also have to keep in mind that although you may have done a chore hundreds of times in the past, your team helpers have not. It is all new to them, and it behooves you to show patience and give them the necessary training and mentoring to gain courage and self-confidence. Walk them through the process and be available to field their questions. Also, a poorly trained helper will make mistakes that will require you to spend time to make frustrating adjustments. The rule of thumb is simple: do proper training and follow-up mentoring so that they get it right the early in the game.

8. **Monitor the delegated tasks closely**: you know well that there will be mistakes, and that difficulties will crop up as your helpers make

progress. You would want to have backup plans, particularly in regard to the consequences of not meeting deadlines or missing out on milestones. The best thing you can do is put out little fires before they become big fires. You would thus want to monitor inexperienced or new team members more so than others. On the positive side, those "first-round" helpers will in time train and monitor their own helpers, thus leaving you twice removed, more or less, from tedious tasks.

9. **Nurture the team's bond with you**: as team leader, the team is your top asset, and if your team is known for its efficiency and includes creative and individuals with great training, then your asset is valued all the more in the company. As a leader, you know how much more you can get from your team if they think highly of you and respect your judgment.

One of the most famous football coaches, Bill Parcells, used to hold friendly one-on-one meetings with team members, asking them for their input, and just making them talk about themselves. He would also invite team members to play pick-up basketball in a relaxed setting where players could view him as a teammate rather than the hard-nosed coach from New York. At first people feared him, but soon enough they ended up revering him.

10. **Time for leadership**: now is the time to show your leadership: when you start delegating, even if only to one person initially, you put yourself on the spot. To rise to the occasion, you need to summon all the virtues of leadership that are essential. For example, the virtue of empathy will tell you to be kind and supportive to your subordinate and to praise them individually as well as publicly with other relevant company staff. The virtue of clarity of thought and voice is evident: you must be well understood. Other traits, such as courage, integrity, passion and awareness, are all characteristics in your persona that will be admired if available for all to see. Leading by example has never been more appropriate, for

your subordinate will hardly work harder for you if they witness behaviors in you that are less than worthy of a leader. Even in a modest way, it would help if your subordinates aspired to emulate you.

~   ~   ~

Chapter Five
Courage & Delegation

Don't let others Shape your Image

Your friends may want you to wear all your emotions on your sleeves, i.e. to show and never suppress your emotions. Feelings that you keep to yourself do not necessarily resonate well with your friends.

Take President Obama for instance: he can be a fiery volcano on the inside, a genuinely passionate man, but because he is "cool" on the outside, people are left to ponder what he's really like. His public relations people thus have to exert additional time and effort to portray him as a gentle and compassionate leader.

In fact, it is not common to find politicians who are outwardly dispassionate. Most politicians who make it on the public stage are typically enthusiastic, backslapping baby kissers who never miss an occasion to show their faces in front of media cameras.

Outward cool is not perceived in terms of "thoughtful" or "thorough", but it is more likely depicted as detached, arrogant or aloof –each one of those with its own set of negative connotations. Thus emotional control and inner courage, traits that have been celebrated in many parts of the globe for thousands of years, seem to have become misunderstood and badly cast in our neck of the woods.

You have to acknowledge though that these norms are not the same in many European or Asian countries, and they are definitely not the same in the military where "cool" is a necessary virtue. You don't get to see a general in sniffles and tears very often.

You May be Delegating Wrong

- You may be doing things wrong if, having worked hard yourself to attain your status and position, and being accustomed to doing things yourself, you now find it difficult to trust and delegate. Your good old self-control and work habits are embedded deeply in your persona, and when there is an important task that needs to be done, you still resort to doing it yourself.

- You may be dumping an assignment on a subordinate and quietly hoping that they can't do it right, thus justifying you to take the assignment back and doing it yourself.

- You may be delegating a task and getting impatient in the middle of seeing it to fruition. You thus take back the task leaving the subordinate confused and dejected.

- Skillful delegation requires empowerment, which in turn requires that you educate your subordinate and give them a proper education on what is required. Empowerment requires that you also motivate your subordinates and assist them wholeheartedly to succeed.

- You may be selecting the wrong person for any given task. Your subordinates cannot possible do well for you if the material you hand down to them is beyond their knowhow and capabilities.

The Courage to Empower

Your courage is a reflection of the fortress inside of you. Aristotle believed courage to be the most important quality in a man. "Courage is the first of human virtues because it makes all others possible." What you can assume he meant is that if you were filled with courage, you would have the guts to exhibit love, compassion and the other virtues –even to appear cool on the outside, if that enhances your resolve and pathway to enlightenment.

Your inner fabric –your courage- is the force that emanates from the sum-total of all your virtues, and it becomes the cornerstone virtue that enables you to face fear and make way for your individual personality to blossom.

You've heard someone being described as having "a backbone like a ramrod and a spine of steel". Well, if you carefully nurture your sense of moral integrity, if you hug the high ground and harness your humanity, your generosity and the other virtues you aspire to live by, then you too could have a backbone like a ramrod and a spine of steel.

It has to be said that half measures are entirely acceptable when embarking on your journey. In other words, you can't hope to genuinely assimilate virtues like that in one swoop. Rather, baby steps are to be encouraged, feeling your way as you move forward. It is not a matter of speed or efficiency but rather one of intellectual conviction and awareness.

You can experience and live by the high moral ground in steps: you first intuitively feel and know what course of action you need to take –seeking purpose- and then your intellect consolidates your feelings. A noble or generous deed is first conceived intuitively –unconsciously- and then your brain highlights what you do and quietly rewards you.

That sequence then becomes one that is subconsciously appealing to you, with the reward at the end. Your acquired nobility and open love become enshrined and part of your nature. And so the story goes, acquiring your other virtues first by intuitively knowing –instinctively- what the right course of action is, and then taking it without a second thought.

In that process, it is you –not others- who chooses the shapes and colors of your image. You get bolder as your self-confidence rises, and as courageous stands become second nature to you.

When it thus comes to delegating to team members in earnest, let your courage guide you towards the better you, the magnanimous, compassionate and resilient you. Have the courage and awareness to know that this will not detract from the most efficient processes or best practices. The more courage you have, the more empowerment you become capable of, and the more benefits accrue to your team members.

But how, apart from your other virtues, do you bolster your courage?

Five Guidelines to Bolster Your Courage

1. **Courage and fear go hand-in-hand**: you ought not to confuse the concept of courage with that of recklessness. Reckless men take unnecessary risks, or ill-calculated risks, whereas "human beings with spines of steel" know how to strike a balance between irrational fear and foolhardiness.

   A man of courage knows spontaneously what ought to be feared. He withstands his fear with confidence, leaning on his sense of honor, nobility and other pillars of morality.

2. **On maintaining a positive mindset**: visualizations (aka imagery) have been found to be extremely useful as aids to staying

positive and coming out ahead at important crossroads.

Athletes who practiced positive imagery and loud affirmations before a contest surpassed others who didn't. "Positive" translates to hope, optimistic, forward looking and other feelings that protect us from sadness, depression and other negative feelings.

You can visualize in your brain any image that strikes you as honorable, and gutsy, e.g. that of your favorite athlete, or even a historical hero of yours such as General Patton or Churchill. You can then turn that into a strong, sometimes loud, affirmation, letting your mind pull you up and turn you into "steel".

3. **Acknowledging your fears**: your shortcomings foster anxieties, and denial breeds fear. It therefore behooves you to learn to live with those shortcomings that you can do nothing about –physical issues for

example, disorders and the like. The sooner you adopt an authentic lifestyle without self-inflicted obstacles, the faster you can be on our way, free of artificial anxieties.

4. **Exposing yourself to vulnerabilities**: it is thought that your self-assessment mechanisms, notably your self-esteem, protect you from your own vulnerabilities. You are instinctively worried that people should see you for who you really are. The remedy is to take the fear out of your vulnerabilities by exposing willfully and persistently that which you always wanted to hide. For example, someone who is short should bring it out into the open, perhaps by joking about it.

5. **Stress is a fierce enemy**: stress is not only tiresome for the mind, but it also diminishes the capabilities of your immune system to fight back against toxins, infections, weariness and fatigue. You need to look out for psychological stress, such as in long-harbored guilt feelings or anger against

parents or others, or for behavioral stress, such as when you are stigmatized or unfairly passed over at work. You know well what the answer to stress is: good nutrition, plenty of sleep, remaining well hydrated, and daily exercise. You shouldn't be surprised that this recipe of clean and active living works wonderfully for your sense of courage.

~   ~   ~

Final Thoughts

Delegating is Liberating

We saw how delegating requires granting authority down the ranks and giving those being delegated the tools, skills and knowledge to be effective and successful. For proper delegating to occur, we also described those two steps as being inseparable. Delegating without empowering is a recipe for failure and anxiety, and part of delegating therefore includes coaching and mentoring, but also the boosting of the empowered person's courage and confidence. Subordinate employees can thus come out feeling liberated and able to look forward with newly gained optimism.

As for managers, the attractive part of delegation is how much time it saves you, and how much opportunity it gives you to shine in pursuit of more demanding areas that are of prime importance to the team as well as the company.

The conclusion therefore is clear: delegating liberates all within the team and, when successful, it creates a culture of collaboration and a sense of being more productive.

Delegation gets you to work more closely with team members, and it is thus a big motivation force in the workplace. When done consistently, delegation grooms people who can replace you altogether. If you are self-confident enough to be comfortable with that prospect, then you are well suited to this process that empowers others.

In this instance, when considering the process of delegation, perfectionists find it extremely difficult to let go of the reins, and when they do, they pick endlessly at the result. They can't let go of even the most trivial chores, and the best advice for that type of manager is to let go of that mindset first, and only then to attempt to delegate.

You are first challenged by the pick you make from among your subordinates in order to delegate a task. If you are timid, you might be swayed by the imagined cry from your helper that would be saying: "Why me?" Naturally, it is important to overcome those kinds of sensitivities and instead explain to the selected subordinate the benefits that they would get from learning additional skills.

Your next hurdle would be in selecting a specific task. Every time you think of one, your mind would also be telling you that it doesn't make sense to let go of that task since "no one can do it better than me". Or, "I don't have time to teach someone on this occasion, so I better do it myself".

Unless you are entirely decisive, your team members will detect your trepidations. You cannot approach someone out of the blue to ask them to do something for you that they've never done before when your words and body language are saying opposing things. You have to be strong, well prepared and convincing, including having freed yourself sufficiently to do a good job introducing your employee to the task to be delegated.

Great leaders empower others routinely and without a fuss. They are viewed as belonging to the "good people" who have great inner fortitude and awareness. They are kind, their empathy boundless, and they invariably become influential mentors. We mentioned the example of the homeless person deriving great pleasure at times from a mere smile or friendly eye contact. If you are to mold yourself into a leadership role, kindness towards others would be one of your most important traits.

Your Inner Fortitude

We also discussed the role of courage and self-confidence in the delegation and empowerment process. Being self-confident is a function of how you view your skills in dealing with whatever circumstances that come your way. This entails how you grade your overall capabilities, although you would also need validation for that self-assessment from society in general and your peers in particular.

In this context you can see the significance of validating your own workers' accomplishments in the workplace. They need you to be generous with your praise and to provide the timely pat on the back. Without that, their self-confidence might wane. That is another mark of a good leader, namely to always be aware and sensitive to his followers' feelings.

We then provided 10 guidelines for enhancing your self-confidence. They are all important and fairly easy to encapsulate into a lifestyle. The fifth guideline we provided is of special importance. It highlights the value of self-love, and it is especially important because many other methods and traits can come out of self-love.

We also listed 10 benefits that accrue from delegating. Guideline number 4, about leadership, stands out, but only for the following reason: empowering others is part of a leader's journey, and when you delegate, you are in effect exercising many of the roles that a leader assumes. For example, you strive to boost employee morale, you speak in terms of positive things and convey hope and optimism, and you think and speak clearly.

If you're going to delegate, you had better delegate the right way. You can't just dump an assignment on an employee and simply hope that they find their way. That would be a recipe for eventual stress and frustration.

Furthermore, you can't just get impatient at a time when your delegated task is being accomplished. Everyone knows that you could have done it in faster time, but you need to give your delegated employee a full and fair chance to get it done, or at least to come and ask you for help.

Finally, when it comes to your courage, keep Aristotle's words in mind as an inspiration: "Courage is the first of human virtues because it makes all others possible." What you can assume from those words is that if you were filled with courage, you would have the guts to exhibit love, compassion and the other virtues –even to appear cool on the outside, if that enhances your resolve and pathway to enlightenment.

Courage therefore ranks with empathy in that they are both marvelous qualities from which overall goodness emanates.

~   ~   ~

Printed in Great Britain
by Amazon

35639149R00037